Let's Read About Insects
LADYBUGS

by Susan Ashley

Reading consultant: Susan Nations, M.Ed., author/literacy coach/consultant

WEEKLY WR READER®
EARLY LEARNING LIBRARY

Please visit our web site at: **www.earlyliteracy.cc**
For a free color catalog describing Weekly Reader® Early Learning Library's
list of high-quality books, call 1-877-445-5824 (USA) or 1-800-387-3178 (Canada).
Weekly Reader® Early Learning Library's fax: (414) 336-0164.

Library of Congress Cataloging-in-Publication Data

Ashley, Susan.
    Ladybugs / by Susan Ashley.
        p. cm. — (Let's read about insects)
    Summary: Brief text describes the appearance, life cycle, reproduction, flight,
and winter hibernation of the colorful insect that benefits farmers and gardeners.
    Includes bibliographical references and index.
    ISBN 0-8368-4055-0 (lib. bdg.)
    ISBN 0-8368-4062-3 (softcover)
    1. Ladybugs—Juvenile literature. (1. Ladybugs.) I. Title.
    QL596.C65A74   2004
    595.76'9—dc22   2003062175

This edition first published in 2004 by
Weekly Reader® Early Learning Library
330 West Olive Street, Suite 100
Milwaukee, WI 53212 USA

Editor: JoAnn Early Macken
Picture research: Diane Laska-Swanke
Art direction and page layout: Tammy Gruenewald

Picture credits: Cover, pp. 5, 7, 9, 11, 13, 15, 17, 21 © Robert & Linda Mitchell;
title © Diane Laska-Swanke; p. 19 © Walt Anderson/Visuals Unlimited

Printed in the United States of America

1 2 3 4 5 6 7 8 9 08 07 06 05 04

Note to Educators and Parents

Reading is such an exciting adventure for young children! They are beginning to integrate their oral language skills with written language. To encourage children along the path to early literacy, books must be colorful, engaging, and interesting; they should invite the young reader to explore both the print and the pictures.

Let's Read About Insects is a new series designed to help children read about insect characteristics, life cycles, and communities. In each book, young readers will learn interesting facts about the featured insects and how they live.

Each book is specially designed to support the young reader in the reading process. The familiar topics are appealing to young children and invite them to read — and reread — again and again. The full-color photographs and enhanced text further support the student during the reading process.

In addition to serving as wonderful picture books in schools, libraries, homes, and other places where children learn to love reading, these books are specifically intended to be read within an instructional guided reading group. This small group setting allows beginning readers to work with a fluent adult model as they make meaning from the text. After children develop fluency with the text and content, the book can be read independently. Children and adults alike will find these books supportive, engaging, and fun!

— Susan Nations, M.Ed., author, literacy coach, and consultant in literacy development

Most people know ladybugs. They are round with black spots. Many ladybugs are red. Some are orange or yellow. Some have two spots, and some have more.

Ladybugs are beetles. A beetle has two hard front wings. These wings cover the beetle's body. They protect its soft back wings.

When a ladybug flies,
its front wings open.
They slide forward.
The ladybug's back
wings can move up
and down.

Not all ladybugs are female. There are male ladybugs, too. Males and females look alike. They mate in spring and summer.

After mating, the female lays eggs. She lays dozens of small yellow eggs on a leaf. When an egg hatches, a **larva** comes out. The larva has six legs. It looks like a caterpillar.

eggs

13

The larva eats and grows. As it grows, it sheds its old skin. After a few weeks, the larva attaches itself to a leaf. It sheds its skin one last time.

The larva turns into a pupa. Inside a hard case, the pupa changes. When it breaks out, it is a fully grown ladybug.

Ladybugs are active all summer. When cold weather comes, they gather in groups. They find a safe place to spend the winter. They **hibernate** until spring.

Farmers and gardeners like ladybugs. They eat insects that harm trees and plants. Are there ladybugs in your yard? What color are they? Can you count their spots?

Glossary

beetle — an insect with four wings. The outer pair protects the inner pair.

caterpillar — the wormlike larva of a butterfly or moth

hibernate — to stop being active for the winter

larva — an insect in its second stage of growth

pupa — an insect in its third stage of growth

For More Information

Books

Posada, Mia. *Ladybugs: Red, Fiery, and Bright*. Minneapolis: Carolrhoda Books, 2002.

Schwartz, David M. *Ladybug*. Milwaukee: Gareth Stevens, 1999.

Tracqui, Valerie. *Face-to-Face with the Ladybug*. Charlesbridge Publishing, 2002.

Web Sites

Discover Learning: Ladybugs

www.discoverlearning.com/webjourneys/ ladybugs/
Ladybug facts and photos

Index

About the Author

Susan Ashley has written over eighteen books for children, including two picture books about dogs, *Puppy Love* and *When I'm Happy, I Smile*. She enjoys animals and writing about them. Susan lives in Wisconsin with her husband and two frisky felines.